COLLEGE BASKETBALL SEASON TICKET

THE ULTIMATE FAN GUIDE

I0895902

BY GRANT MITCHELL

First Edition
First Printing, 2019

Book design by Sarah Taplin
Cover design by Sarah Taplin
Photographs ©: Mark J. Terrill/AP Images, cover (top), 92; Brian Rothmuller/Icon Sportswire/AP Images, cover (left); Scott Kinser/Cal Sport Media/AP Images, cover (middle right); Mark Humphrey/AP Images, cover (bottom right), 64, 67; Brynn Anderson/AP Images, 4; Ben McKeown/AP Images, 8; Eric Gay/AP Images, 10–11; AP Images, 12, 20, 33, 36, 39, 56, 68, 75, 80; Matty Zimmerman/AP Images, 15; Chris Steppig/NCAA Photos/AP Images, 18; Jim Mone/AP Images, 23; Zach Bolinger/Icon Sportswire, 27; Ryan Kang/AP Images, 28; Elise Amendola/AP Images, 35; Bill Kostroun/AP Images, 42; Chuck Burton/AP Images, 45; The Virginian-Pilot/AP Images, 46; Lennox McLendon/AP Images, 49; Amy Sancetta/AP Images, 53; Tony Gutierrez/AP Images, 55; Orlin Wagner/AP Images, 62; Darron Cummings/AP Images, 72; Aaron Suozzi/AP Images, 76; Ron Schwane/AP Images, 85; Michael Conroy/AP Images, 86; Sean Rayford/AP Images, 95

Design Elements ©: Pixabay

Press Box Books, an imprint of Press Room Editions.

Library of Congress Control Number: 2018952205

ISBN:
978-1-63494-055-9 (paperback)
978-1-63494-067-2 (epub)
978-1-63494-079-5 (hosted ebook)

Distributed by North Star Editions, Inc.
2297 Waters Drive
Mendota Heights, MN 55120
www.northstareditions.com

Printed in the United States of America

TABLE OF CONTENTS

NATIONAL
VILLANOVA
WILDCATS
CHAMPIONS
WERNER

CHAPTER 1

OPENING TIP

The final buzzer sounded. The crowd at the Alamodome in San Antonio, Texas, let out a cheer. With a 79–62 win over Michigan, the Villanova Wildcats had won the 2018 National Collegiate Athletic Association (NCAA) men's basketball tournament. The celebration was on.

Finally, with the confetti having fallen, the interviews wrapped up, and the trophies handed out, only one task remained. As fans cheered them on, the Villanova players climbed a ladder. One by one they snipped pieces of the basketball net. At last, junior guard Mikal Bridges ascended the ladder and, with one final cut, removed the last piece of the net.

"It's just the best feeling," said Bridges, who scored 19 points in the win.

Villanova's Mikal Bridges waves the net in celebration after winning the 2018 men's national title.

To an outsider, this celebration might seem strange. But for college basketball players—both men and women—there's nothing quite like cutting down a net. College teams have been doing it since 1947. Now this tradition is as much a part of a big win as the final buzzer. Whether it's a conference title, a berth in the Final Four, or a national championship, chances are the night ends with a ladder and scissors.

"When we go into a gym where there is net-cutting involved," said Stanford women's coach Tara VanDerveer, "I tell our team right away: 'Look at those nets. Do whatever it takes to get those nets because that's what we're here for.'"

She would know. Through 2018, VanDerveer had led her teams to two national titles and 12 Final Fours.

Basketball is played at all levels, from city parks to the pros to the Olympics. People around the world play and watch the game, whether they're in Canada or China, or Arkansas or Australia. Of all the levels of basketball, however, college basketball is special. The traditions, such as cutting down the nets after a big win, are a big reason.

College basketball doesn't claim to be the best. That's what the National Basketball Association (NBA) and Women's National Basketball Association (WNBA) are for. But college offers passion and traditions that the pros can't match. Players represent their schools. Students fill the arenas and cheer loudly for the entire game. And with only four years of eligibility for athletes, every moment counts.

The moments in the single-elimination NCAA Tournament, however, might count just a little bit more.

Rivalries are a huge part of college basketball. And no men's rivalry can quite match that of Duke and North Carolina. This one has it all. The schools are only 10 miles apart on Tobacco Road. Duke is a private university, whereas North Carolina is public. And both teams are among the most successful in the sport's history. So when Duke is preparing to host North Carolina, the home fans camp out for days just to get tickets.

Though it's one of the most famous arenas in the sport, Duke's Cameron Indoor Stadium seats only 9,000 fans. Those students lucky enough to get into the stadium join the Cameron Crazies fan section. Dressed in all blue, they make the arena one of the most difficult places to play.

Duke fans ensure North Carolina players never get comfortable when visiting Cameron Indoor Stadium.

On the women's side, Connecticut and Tennessee defined the sport for years. These schools don't have much in common on paper. Instead, they're bound together by excellence.

Tennessee coach Pat Summitt set the standard for a successful women's program during the 1980s and 1990s. Then UConn's Geno Auriemma built a program that could match it. Their games captivated fans around the country. From 1995 to 2007, the schools met 22 times. During those years they combined for nine NCAA titles. Though Tennessee took a step back after Summitt retired in 2012, power programs such as Stanford and Notre Dame have stepped up to challenge the Huskies in recent years.

While games between the nation's top programs always attract attention, it's the regional rivalries that really drive the sport all across the country. There's Duke-North Carolina, Louisville-Kentucky, Indiana-Purdue, Kansas-Missouri, Georgetown-Villanova, Arizona-UCLA, and many more. Rivalry games matter, regardless of how good the teams are that season.

The NBA might have new state-of-the-art arenas, but college basketball's barns have the history. The Palestra, located in Philadelphia, at the University of Pennsylvania, is known as the Cathedral of College Basketball. It opened in 1927 and has played host to more college games and visiting teams than any other venue. One year later, Butler University opened its arena, now known as Hinkle Fieldhouse, in Indianapolis, Indiana. For two decades, it stood as the largest basketball arena in the country, and the climactic scenes of the 1986 movie *Hoosiers* were

Confetti falls on the South Carolina women's team after they won the 2017 national title.

filmed there. Allen Fieldhouse in Kansas has been around since 1955. If you go see a game there, you'll hear fans recite an even older chant: "Rock Chalk, Jayhawk, KU!"

However, no tradition in American sports can quite compare with the Division I NCAA Tournaments. With 68 teams on the men's side and 64 on the women's, these events have rightly earned the nickname "March

Madness." In the tournaments, schools big and small, public and private, from big cities and small towns, all play for the title. With a single-elimination format, every game is vital—and there are upsets aplenty. Teams and players cement their legacies in the tournament. At the end of the crazy month, only one team remains . . . and that team gets to cut down the nets as college basketball champions.

CHAPTER 2

THE MEN TIP OFF

The history of basketball is college basketball. It was at Springfield College in 1891 that James Naismith nailed two peach baskets to the wall of a gym and called the sport "basket ball." The first game that day in Massachusetts didn't look much like the basketball of today. There were nine players per team, and the final score was 1–0.

But the sport quickly gained popularity. Hundreds of people started coming out to watch games. Students at the college brought the game back home with them, and it spread around the country. By 1895, the first intercollegiate basketball game took place in Minnesota. Using Naismith's "peach basket" rules, Hamline College beat the Minnesota State School of Agriculture 9–3. All of the players were men.

After inventing basketball, James Naismith coached the Kansas men's team.

The game quickly grew from there. By the turn of the century, there were 45 schools playing college basketball. In 10 years, that number had tripled. Conferences were starting to pop up, too, in order to organize teams into leagues.

For the first half of the 20th century, college basketball was the top echelon of the sport. Pro leagues did exist, but none lasted until the NBA formed in 1948. At the same time, college basketball was mostly regional. Although conferences determined their champions, there was no true national tournament.

The National Invitation Tournament (NIT) changed that. Seen today as a consolation prize, the NIT began as the original national championship. The tournament was first held in 1938. For that first NIT, organizers invited six teams to New York City, where Temple took down Colorado 60–36 to win the title. The NIT was a huge success. In fact, it was so successful that the NCAA started its own tournament the next year. Both continue to this day.

Early on, the NIT was seen as the more prestigious tournament. The NCAA Tournament gradually surpassed the NIT in significance. In 1950, however, the two tournaments ended on equal footing. That's

CCNY's Ed Roman goes for a basket against Kentucky during the 1950 NIT.

because tiny City College of New York (CCNY) stunned the basketball world by winning both the NIT and the NCAA Tournament.

That historic moment soon became one that the sport's officials would rather forget. Seven CCNY players were involved in a series of scandals that included fixing the results of games. The scandal crushed CCNY basketball, which dropped to Division III in 1963.

Despite the scandal, college basketball was booming in popularity nationally. In 1954, NBC paid

$7,500 for the rights to air the first nationally televised college basketball game, a sizable amount at the time.

It was that same year that the shot clock was introduced in the NBA. But the college game didn't adopt the shot clock until 1985. In fact, college basketball in general saw few on-court changes throughout the 20th century. Whereas the NBA made changes to increase scoring and general excitement, the college game emphasized the traditional game play of the time. Even dunking was banned in college games from 1967 to 1976.

Eventually the college game began catching up to the pro rules. A year after the shot clock came the three-point line. It changed the game immediately. In that first season with the three, the Providence Friars made a run to the Final Four, attempting 665 three-pointers while their opponents took 349. It also helped that the Friars hit 42.1 percent of theirs, whereas their opponents hit a paltry 31.2 percent.

Hitting three-pointers became a vital part of college basketball, and teams raced to catch up. But adding the arc changed college basketball beyond only one scoring play. College basketball had been a big man's game, where centers would battle it out underneath the baskets. But the three-pointer opened up all that. With the three-pointer, teams that lacked size now had another weapon in their arsenals.

While the shot clock and three-point line changed how teams play the game, off-court changes have had huge effects, too. Perhaps the biggest was the 2005 addition of the "one-and-done" rule.

In the early days of the NBA Draft, players had to be out of high school for four years to be eligible—essentially requiring a player to attend college. That changed in 1971. After one year in college, Spencer Haywood signed with the Denver Rockets of the American Basketball Association (ABA), where he was the league's 1969–70 Rookie of the Year. Then the NBA's Seattle SuperSonics offered him a deal, which he could not accept due to NBA rules. So Hayward challenged the NBA's rule in the US Supreme Court, and the league was forced to change its rule.

But even after the Haywood decision, NBA teams in practice rarely drafted high school players. Moses Malone and Darryl Dawkins were two notable exceptions. Then, in 1995, Kevin Garnett changed everything. The power forward from Chicago's Farragut Career Academy declared for that year's NBA

In his lone college season, Anthony Davis led Kentucky to the 2012 men's national title.

Draft. This began a major influx of high school talent to the NBA that included Kobe Bryant and LeBron James during the next 10 years.

Some of these high school players thrived. Many others flamed out. By 2005, owners and executives decided they were too often getting burned on high school lottery tickets. The teams wanted more time and more data to evaluate players. So starting with the 2006 draft, only players ages 19 and older and one year removed from high school were eligible to be selected.

This meant the top high school seniors now had a year to kill before they could declare for the draft, and most of them spent that year playing in the NCAA. This created what's known as one-and-done. Players such as Greg Oden of Ohio State and Derrick Rose of Memphis led their schools to the brink of a national championship, and then left for the greener pastures of the NBA. Before long, all of the top programs were going after these one-and-done players.

Building teams around freshmen, no matter their talent, isn't always a winning formula. Sometimes they lack the experience or maturity to lead a team. They might struggle against veteran teams with a lot of experience playing together. But top programs still covet these one-and-done players.

No school has thrived in the one-and-done era quite like Kentucky. Under coach John Calipari, the Wildcats routinely fill their roster with one-year players. And each year they manage to come together to make a formidable team, with the 2012 squad winning the national title.

904

CHAPTER 3

THE WOMEN'S GAME FOLLOWS

Women's basketball can also trace its history back to a college. And the women's game is nearly as old as the men's. It started with Senda Berenson. She was the director of physical education at Smith College, an all-women's school in Northampton, Massachusetts. In 1893, she read about the new sport of "basket ball" and thought it might be a fit for her students.

Berenson met James Naismith at a conference in 1893. Though women at the time were discouraged from playing team sports, Naismith encouraged her to try the sport as a form of exercise for her students.

A group of women play basketball at Smith College during the 1940s.

The rules were modified specifically for women. Berenson thought playing a full-court game would be too tiring for women players. So the Berenson rules called for six players per team, and the court was divided into three sections. Players could not leave their assigned section. This limited the amount of running they had to do.

On March 22, 1893, Berenson organized the first official women's college basketball game. Smith's sophomores faced off against the freshmen. By 1896, the first intercollegiate game took place. Stanford and Cal played each other in Berkeley, California.

Women's basketball had quickly expanded from one coast to the other. However, the sport lacked formal organization for decades. In fact, for much of that time any women's sport that required excessive physical exertion was shunned across the country. Because of that, opportunities for most women's sports were severely limited.

It wasn't until the 1970s that everything began to change. The Association for Intercollegiate Athletics for Women (AIAW) formed in 1971. It organized women's sports, whereas the NCAA focused on men. This brought formal oversight to women's basketball and other sports. And so it was only then that women

A Delta State player dribbles against Louisiana State during the 1977 AIAW title game.

officially began playing five-a-side, full-court games like the men. The AIAW also introduced a 30-second shot clock. That put the women's game ahead of the men in adopting that rule.

Then, in 1972, all women's sports in the United States were tremendously boosted. That year marked the passage of Title IX. It guaranteed girls and women equal opportunities in schools. This included sports. So if a school wanted to give athletic scholarships to men, it now had to offer an equal number of athletic scholarships to women, too. This has gradually led to a massive increase in opportunities and participation for girls' and women's sports.

That year also marked a major milestone for women's college basketball. The AIAW held its first national tournament. One of the competing teams was the Tennessee-Martin Skyhawks. An All-American named Patricia Head starred for that team. She would later become Tennessee coach Pat Summitt. However, it was tiny Immaculata College that won the title, overcoming previously unbeaten West Chester State 52–48 in the title game.

Immaculata's "Mighty Macs" were an early dynasty, winning the first three national titles. Their third came in New York City's Madison Square Garden. Approximately 12,000 fans watched from the arena, and the game was televised nationally. At its peak, the AIAW counted nearly 1,000 member schools among its ranks.

For a time, men's and women's college sports programs were mostly separate. That eventually changed. By the early 1980s, more women's programs had joined the NCAA. That organization held its first women's championship tournament in 1982.

That proved to be a year of transition. Rutgers won the 1982 AIAW championship, becoming the final champions from that organization. The defending

AIAW champs, meanwhile, had jumped to the NCAA. Louisiana Tech ran roughshod over the NCAA competition in 1981–82. The Lady Techsters lost only one game and never fell from their No. 1 ranking. They were barely troubled in the tournament, topping Cheyney State in the title game. Among Louisiana Tech's stars was point guard Kim Mulkey, who would later lead Baylor to the 2005 and 2012 national titles as a coach.

Instead of earning championship rings, as is the custom today, the Lady Techsters earned watches. For the 35th anniversary of their title, that slight was corrected. The NCAA finally presented the team members with their championship rings.

Louisiana Tech proved to be the dominant team of the era. The Lady Techsters were runners-up in 1983 and 1987, and then they added a second NCAA title in 1988. One coach who tired of running into the Lady Techsters was Summitt, by then leading the Tennessee Lady Volunteers.

Summitt had coached Tennessee since 1974. Almost immediately, she built the Lady Vols into a national title contender, first in the AIAW and then in the NCAA. They lost to the Lady Techsters in the 1982 Final Four.

It wasn't long until Summitt turned the Lady Vols into a dynasty. They won their first national title in 1987, another in 1989, and a third in 1991. They became even more dominant in the 1990s. Tennessee became the first women's team to win three straight NCAA titles, doing so from 1996 to 1998. The 1997–98 squad also went 39–0.

In 2000, Summitt was named the Naismith Coach of the Century. But she was far from done. The Vols went on to win two more national titles before Summitt retired in 2012. She did so with 1,098 career wins, the most in Division I history for a woman or a man. Her success as a coach helped boost the entire sport. So did Tennessee's rivalry with Connecticut.

Almost immediately after coach Geno Auriemma took over as UConn coach in 1985, the Huskies became contenders. They made the NCAA Tournament in 1989, and through 2018 they hadn't missed a tournament since. For a time, particularly in the 1990s and early 2000s, any UConn-Tennessee game was a must-see event.

UConn won its first national title in 1995, and by the 2000s the Huskies were nearly unbeatable. UConn won 10 national titles from 2000 to 2016,

UConn's Breanna Stewart ended her college career in 2016 with four national titles in four years.

five of them in undefeated seasons. In the middle of winning four titles in a row from 2013 to 2016, UConn reeled off a record 111-game winning streak. Starting on November 23, 2014, the Huskies didn't lose again until the 2017 Final Four.

Although UConn remained a force, that loss signaled a minor sea change in the women's college basketball landscape. In 2017, South Carolina topped Mississippi State for the national championship. That was the first time there were two brand-new participants in the national title game since 2005. It was a sign that the women's game was as strong as ever, and it continued to grow.

N.C.A.A.

CHAPTER 4

MARCH MADNESS

Take a look at the Final Four from the first men's NCAA Tournament in 1939, and it looks pretty familiar. Ohio State, Oregon, Villanova, and Oklahoma reached the national semifinals, with Oregon winning it all. But compared with the full stadiums, national television audiences, and 68-team bracket of today, that first tournament could not have been more different.

The 1939 tournament consisted of eight teams battling it out at the Patten Gymnasium in Evanston, Illinois. Despite being much closer to home, Ohio State fell to the then-Oregon Webfoots 46–33 in the championship game. The game wasn't televised, but Oregon fans were thrilled nonetheless. They prepared a hero's welcome for their boys when they returned to Eugene on the train three days later.

Oregon beat Ohio State to win this trophy in the first NCAA Tournament in 1939.

Illinois was a natural choice to host the first NCAA Tournament. Its high school basketball tournament had already been wildly popular for years. In fact, it was Henry V. Porter, the assistant executive secretary of the Illinois High School Association, who first came up with the term "March Madness." Seeing the excitement for the state's 1939 high school basketball tournament, he wrote an essay about how much fans looked forward to it each year.

A "little March madness may complement and contribute to sanity and help keep society on an even keel," wrote Porter, who would later be inducted into the Basketball Hall of Fame. The phrase endured. Porter used it again in a 1942 poem called "Basketball Ides of March." "The Madness of March is running," it said. "The winged feet fly, the ball sails high. . . ."

For decades, the only tournament associated with "March Madness" was the Illinois high school tournament. It wasn't until the 1980s that the term became synonymous with the NCAA Tournament. The name generally coincided with the expansion of the men's NCAA Tournament to 64 teams in 1985.

One game in particular is often credited with sparking the college game's popularity. In 1979, the country had two superstars. Earvin "Magic" Johnson was a talented sophomore point guard at Michigan State. Meanwhile, senior forward Larry Bird was practically a one-man show at Indiana State. When the teams met in that year's NCAA title game, it brought attention never before seen at the college level. Fans around the country tuned in to see Johnson and Michigan State win that year's title.

The tournament continued growing into the 1980s, thanks in part to expended TV coverage from new cable channels. For most of the tournament's history, few, if any, games were shown on TV. Sometimes, even the games that were televised were tape delayed. Going to 64 teams also increased excitement. The upsets were bigger, and the Cinderella stories were more impressive.

Another way fans engaged with the tournament was by filling out their own bracket and entering contests to see who could guess the most winners. Until the 64-team format was created, filling out a bracket could be complicated. In the 1950s, for example, 23 teams made the field, and there were nine byes to go around.

The tournament also tended to be more predictable at times. During the 1960s and 1970s, California-Los Angeles—better known as UCLA—dominated, at one point winning 10 of 12 titles. For anyone who wasn't a Bruins fan, the tournament didn't hold much interest.

But that had changed by the 1980s. More teams meant more action and more excitement. Few could believe it when North Carolina State won the 1983 title as a No. 6 seed. Two years later, in 1985, the first year with 64 teams, No. 8 Villanova upset reigning national champs and top-seeded Georgetown to win its first title. Then in 1988, the upstart Kansas Jayhawks won it all despite having one of the worst records ever for a national champion at 21–11.

The 1980s were a time of great growth for the women's NCAA Tournament as well. After the first one in 1982, the tournament grew in national popularity quickly. The first women's tournament consisted of 32 teams, but that grew to 40 within four years and to 48 by 1989. It has been at 64 teams since 1994.

While many players have put together dominating college careers, the best-known players are often ones who show up the most in March.

Before Steph Curry was a superstar for the Golden State Warriors, he was a little-known guard from Davidson, which played in a mid-major conference. As the son of a former NBA player, Curry had received

North Carolina State's Lorenzo Charles dunks to seal the 1983 NCAA title.

some attention as a great shooter. But when he led Davidson to the 2008 Elite Eight, he became a household name. Curry averaged 32 points per game in leading the Wildcats to within one game of the Final Four, losing to eventual national champion Kansas.

Kemba Walker put up one of the greatest performances in men's tournament history in 2011. In leading the UConn Huskies to the national title, Walker averaged 23.5 points, 6.0 rebounds, and 5.7 assists per game. He played almost every minute in UConn's six-game run to the title.

Kentucky became infamous for its one-and-done players in the 2010s. One of its greatest success stories was Anthony Davis, whose physical presence carried the Wildcats to the 2012 title. Davis was a beast, averaging 13.7 points, 12.3 rebounds, 4.8 blocks, and 3.0 assists per game in the tournament.

Texas Tech's Sheryl Swoopes had maybe the best performance in the history of the women's tournament. She scored 47 points in the 1993 national championship game against Ohio State. She was 16-of-24 from the field and hit all 11 of her free throws in leading the Red Raiders to the national title.

Sometimes the performances can come out of nowhere. Morgan William scored 41 points for Mississippi State in its 2017 Elite Eight matchup with Baylor. William was averaging only approximately 10 points per game in the regular season. Standing just 5-foot-5, she hit 6-of-8 threes while also running the

Sheryl Swoopes celebrates winning the 1993 national title with Texas Tech.

offense from the point. Then, one game later, she hit the buzzer-beater that snapped UConn's 111-game winning streak.

Even though it's only one tournament, these players will be remembered forever because it's March Madness, and each one is special.

U.S.F.
6
U.S.F.
19

CHAPTER 5

THE ICONIC MEN

College sports teams turn over quickly. Players have only four years of eligibility, and many of the best leave sooner than that. So college sports fans are used to rooting for the name on the front of the jersey, as the names on the back are constantly changing. Some special players, however, are too good to forget.

The University of San Francisco (USF) is not known as a college basketball power. But in the 1950s, the school had a bit of luck. Across the bay, a young center named Bill Russell became an all-conference player at McClymonds High School in Oakland, California. USF offered him a scholarship. With no other offers, Russell accepted and turned USF into a force.

During his first season, in 1953–54, Russell averaged 20 points per game. But he was even more

USF's Bill Russell dunks against St. Mary's in a 1956 game.

renowned on defense, using his imposing size to block shots and gather rebounds. Behind Russell, USF won back-to-back national championships in 1955 and 1956. They remain the only two national titles in school history.

After college, Russell proved himself to be the sport's greatest winner. He also won the 1956 Olympic gold medal with Team USA, plus 11 NBA titles with the Boston Celtics.

Another player who used his size to dominate the college ranks was Lew Alcindor (later Kareem Abdul-Jabbar). Alcindor stood 7-foot-2 as a freshman at UCLA, a towering height in any league. Freshmen were not allowed to play on college varsity teams yet. But in his first varsity game in 1966, Alcindor dropped 56 points against rival Southern Cal (USC).

In fact, Alcindor was so big and so dominant that the NCAA tried to slow him down by banning the slam dunk. As it turned out, the rule didn't slow him at all. In response, Alcindor developed his trademark "skyhook." With Alcindor easily rising above opponents, the shot was almost impossible to defend. At UCLA, Alcindor won national championships all three seasons, from 1967 to 1969.

Lew Alcindor scored lots of points for UCLA with his iconic "skyhook" shot.

Following in Alcindor's huge footsteps at UCLA was another dominant big man, Bill Walton. Besides his physical presence, Walton was noted as a student of the game and a free spirit. A native of Southern California, he brought the same intensity to the court as he did to his personal life, even being arrested at an anti-Vietnam War rally during his junior year.

On the basketball court, few won as much as Walton. His high school team went undefeated in his senior year. Then the highly recruited center was on back-to-back 30–0 teams in his first two years at UCLA. By the time the winning streak ended on January 19, 1974, Walton had been on the winning team for 129 consecutive games. He also won three NCAA titles. The curly-haired center was a big reason for all of those wins. He broke Alcindor's UCLA record for rebounds during his three seasons in Westwood. He also shot 65.1 percent from the field. Injuries slowed Walton's NBA career, but he went down as one of the most dominant college players of all time.

Of all the great college big men, Ralph Sampson may have been the greatest—and the best. Standing 7-foot-4, Sampson dominated college basketball in the 1980s. He and Walton are still the only players to have won three Naismith Player of the Year Awards. But Sampson's career was overshadowed by losses. His Virginia Cavaliers made only one Final Four. And they were part of one of the greatest upsets in college basketball history, when Division II Chaminade beat them on December 23, 1982.

Sometimes stardom and tragedy collide. Len Bias was an All-American for Maryland in 1986. He was also the Atlantic Coast Conference (ACC) Player of the Year, averaging 23 points and seven rebounds per game. However, the day after the Boston Celtics drafted him second overall, Bias died of an accidental drug overdose.

Another tragic case was that of Hank Gathers. The power forward from Loyola Marymount led the nation in both scoring and rebounding in 1989–90. The Lions were having their best season in history when Gathers suffered a heart attack on the court. He collapsed and died during that game in the West Coast Conference Tournament. Through 2018, Loyola Marymount hadn't been back to the NCAA Tournament since.

Although many college basketball stars were beloved by fans, others became known as the sport's great villains. No player represented the love-hate

Whether loved or hated, fans couldn't help but respect Christian Laettner's production for Duke.

relationship quite like Duke's Christian Laettner. From 1989 to 1992, the forward played in 23 NCAA Tournament games. The most one player could possibly play during that period was 24. In other words, Laettner's teams won, a lot.

Laettner was a big reason for all that winning. He shot 57.4 percent from the floor for his career and averaged 7.8 rebounds per game. During his senior year, nearly every organization that named a player of the year gave the award to Laettner.

For all of his success, Laettner is best remembered for one play. With overtime winding down in the 1992 Elite Eight, Duke trailed Kentucky by one point. That's when Duke called an audacious play. Inbounding the ball from under his own basket with 2.1 seconds to play, Grant Hill sent a long pass to Laettner, who caught it atop the Wildcats' key. Laettner took a dribble, turned, and swished the game-winner. Duke went on to win the national title, its second in a row.

Years later, the actor Rob Lowe directed a documentary called *I Hate Christian Laettner*. He believed fans loved to hate Laettner because he was "a massively talented pretty boy who takes no (crap) from anyone."

Of course, no fan base dislikes Duke as much as neighboring North Carolina. The Tar Heels have had their share of iconic players through the years, such as Michael Jordan in the 1980s and Vince Carter in the 1990s. From 2006 to 2009, however, Tyler Hansbrough set a new standard.

The power forward was aggressive on both ends of the floor, often irritating opponents into making a mistake. His energetic play helped him sweep all of the 2009 player of the year awards. He then led the Tar Heels to the national championship. No ACC player had scored more than Hansbrough's 2,872 career points. He also set a team record with 1,219 rebounds.

"There will never be another one just like him," coach Roy Williams said.

These are only a few of the all-time greats of college basketball. With the increase of one-and-done players since the late 1990s, the game has changed slightly. Fewer players are putting together standout four-year careers, so what defines a great career has shifted. Instead, players like Carmelo Anthony at Syracuse or Anthony Davis at Kentucky cement their status with unforgettable freshman seasons, and then they're off to the NBA.

Due to his endless energy, North Carolina's Tyler Hansbrough (top) was nicknamed "Psycho T."

22
Monarchs

CHAPTER 6

THE ICONIC WOMEN

With feisty defense and sharp passing, Nancy Lieberman knew how to control a game. As a junior in 1979, she led Old Dominion, in Virginia, to the 1979 AIAW championship. Then, during Lieberman's senior year, a 6-foot-8 center named Anne Donovan joined the Lady Monarchs.

"We had a certain level of excellence, and we wanted her to rise to that occasion," Lieberman said. "Plus nobody wants the new kid on the block to get all the attention and the hype. We were like, 'If you're that good, prove it.'"

Did she ever.

Anne Donovan's arrival at Old Dominion helped cement the school as a power in women's basketball.

Donovan and Lieberman led Old Dominion to a second AIAW title in 1980. Then, with Lieberman gone, Donovan took the Lady Monarchs back to two more Final Fours. For her career, she averaged 20 points, 14.5 rebounds, and 5.9 blocks per game. Her 801 career blocks remain a national record.

"Annie was so quiet and kind, but she was such a competitor," Lieberman said. "She didn't have to brag. She just did her business, and everywhere she went, she won."

Donovan and Lieberman went on to win two Olympic gold medals together with Team USA. Both are in the Basketball Hall of Fame, too. And they were just at the beginning of a parade of dominant women.

The 1980s proved to be an important time for many women's sports in the United States. For the first time, young women showing up on college campuses had grown up during the Title IX era. As kids, they had played at a time when girls' sports participation was rapidly rising. And with greater opportunities at the youth levels, women emerged as bigger stars during the 1980s. The arrival of the NCAA Tournament in 1982 gave them a platform on which to shine.

As good as Donovan was with Old Dominion, Janice Lawrence and Cheryl Miller were making names for

Cheryl Miller (center) celebrates with teammate Cynthia Cooper (right) after winning the 1984 NCAA title.

themselves, too. Lawrence arrived at Louisiana Tech in 1981. In the course of four years, the forward averaged 17.8 points per game for the Lady Techsters. One year after leading the team to the 1981 AIAW title, Lawrence was named MVP in leading the team to the first NCAA title in 1982.

Then Miller took over. As a high school player in Riverside, California, she once scored 105 points in a game. That scoring prowess continued in college at USC. The forward finished her four-year career by tallying 3,018 points. Alongside teammate Cynthia

Cooper, Miller helped turn USC into a power. The Trojans won back-to-back NCAA titles in 1983 and 1984, with Miller being named Naismith College Player of the Year three times.

Another set of stars broke out in the early part of the 1990s. Lisa Leslie became a household name during her four-year career at USC. The 6-foot-5 center played a different game than the slashing Miller, but the points stacked up all the same. Leslie averaged 20.1 points per game during her career with the Trojans. That led to a decorated career in the WNBA, which began in 1997.

Sheryl Swoopes became another WNBA superstar. First, though, she was a force for Texas Tech. A 6-foot wing player, Swoopes was often compared to NBA superstar Michael Jordan, and for good reason. At no point was she more dominant than in the 1993 NCAA title game against Ohio State.

"At a point in the game, I just felt I wanted to take control," Swoopes said. "I felt like I wanted to score every time I got the ball."

Indeed, she made 16 fields goals and went 11-for-11 on free throws. No matter what the Buckeyes tried to throw at her defensively, Swoopes answered. Her 47 points in that game was an NCAA title game record for both women and men. More important, it helped the Red Raiders win 84–82.

"You don't really appreciate Sheryl Swoopes until you have to stop her," said Ohio State coach Nancy Darsch. "She hurt us, not just by the scoring. I saw us get a little down, a little dejected when she scored some tough shots against us. She attacked our heart."

With Title IX in full effect and the WNBA beginning, women's basketball reached the next level in the late 1990s. A big reason for that was two programs that kept raising the bar. The Tennessee Lady Volunteers raised it higher than ever. Behind Chamique Holdsclaw and Tamika Catchings, the Lady Vols won three consecutive national championships from 1996 to 1998. With six NCAA titles at the time, Tennessee was the clear power in women's basketball.

> "You don't really appreciate Sheryl Swoopes until you have to stop her."
>
> –Ohio State coach Nancy Darsch

Then a series of dominant players at Connecticut had something to say about that. In 1995, center Rebecca Lobo led UConn to its first national title. Able to make shots from both inside and the perimeter, she averaged nearly 17 points per game. That opened the door for more Huskies to continue the tradition. After Lobo, point guard Sue Bird took over for UConn, leading the Huskies to the 2000 and 2002 national titles. Bird could score, pass, and defend, averaging nearly 12 points and five assists to go with two steals per game.

Next came Diana Taurasi. She one-upped Bird, ending her career by winning three consecutive national titles. A 6-foot guard, Taurasi was a sharpshooter who averaged 15 points, 4.3 rebounds, and 4.5 assists per game.

Taurasi also helped turn the tables in the Tennessee-UConn rivalry. Behind two-time national player of the year Holdsclaw, the Lady Vols won four of six games against the Huskies. But with Taurasi, the Huskies were 6–1 against Tennessee heading into their 2004 NCAA title game meeting.

"She's a great player," Tennessee forward LaToya Davis said before that game. "She's just awesome. I admire her game because she gets everybody involved. . . . She's going to get her points and she's going to get her teammates open. We just need to try to contain her."

Sue Bird (left) and Diana Taurasi set a new standard at UConn during the early 2000s.

The Lady Vols did their best, holding Taurasi to 18 points, but the All-American was still able to lead her team to a convincing 81–67 win.

That win ushered in a new era. Though forward Candace Parker and the Vols won championships in 2007 and 2008, UConn proved to be the sport's biggest power in years to come. Another dominant generation of players followed Taurasi, led by small forward Maya Moore and center Tina Charles. They helped the Huskies win back-to-back titles in 2009 and 2010. Breanna Stewart continued the tradition. She guided the Huskies to a record 111-game winning streak as well as national titles each of her four seasons, from 2013 to 2016. In total, UConn won 10 championships from 2000 to 2016.

The stars of the 2000s weren't limited to Connecticut, though. Although they never won a national title, Alana Beard often had her Duke team in the national title picture during the early 2000s. She averaged nearly 20 points per game and became the first women's player to have her number retired at Duke.

Meanwhile, Seimone Augustus and Louisiana State (LSU) mounted a challenge to Tennessee in the Southeastern Conference. From 2002 to 2006, Augustus averaged 22.7 points per game. That made her the top scorer in the country as she led the Tigers to three Final Fours.

Back on the East Coast, 6-foot-5 forward Elena Delle Donne emerged in a nontraditional way. First, she spurned UConn to attend college closer to home at Delaware, not exactly a powerhouse sports school. Then she decided to play volleyball, not basketball, citing burnout. When she finally did join the basketball team in 2009, she quickly became a star. Delle Donne averaged more than 26 points per game, leading the Blue Hens to three NCAA Tournaments.

Brittney Griner was a dominant presence in the post during her years at Baylor.

Down south, Brittney Griner took over the sport in a different way. Towering over opponents at 6-foot-9, the center led Baylor to the 2012 national title. A force in the paint, Griner put up 3,283 points in her career.

And out west, Kelsey Plum was making her own mark on the sport. In 2017, Plum finished off her career at Washington by becoming the leading scorer in NCAA women's basketball history. She finished with 3,527 points and shot 53 percent from the field.

This wealth of superstar players shows that, despite its start, women's basketball is as strong as ever, and it's only growing.

CCNY
7

CHAPTER 7

UNFORGETTABLE TEAMS

Winning a national championship is something players and fans will never forget. But certain teams are special. Whether it's a run of dominance, a unique cast of characters, or just an unforgettable season, these teams rise above the rest in the sport's history.

In 1950, the CCNY men's team made history. After finishing a strong regular season, the Beavers received the last spot in the NIT. At the time, making the NIT was a higher honor than making the NCAA Tournament. Playing in its own backyard at Madison Square Garden in New York City, CCNY stunned USF, the top seed in the tournament. The Beavers

The CCNY players lift coach Nat Holman in celebration after winning the 1950 NCAA title in New York City.

eventually went on to win the NIT as they knocked off Bradley in the championship game.

Shortly after CCNY captured the NIT crown, the Beavers were once again an underdog as they were the last team selected to the NCAA Tournament. Back at Madison Square Garden, CCNY made another run. In the end, the Beavers became the only team ever to win both the NIT and NCAA Tournaments in the same season.

As time went on, the NCAA Tournament took over as the top tournament in college basketball. The 1955–56 USF Dons captured the crown with some of the game's all-time greats. The Dons won both the 1955 and 1956 NCAA championships behind legends Bill Russell and K. C. Jones. Their strong play led to San Francisco being the first school in NCAA history to complete a perfect season.

In the early 1960s, men's college basketball's longest-running dynasty began. John Wooden arrived at UCLA in 1948 and began building the Bruins into an all-time powerhouse. In 1962, UCLA made it to the national semifinals before falling to eventual champion Cincinnati. In 1964, Wooden and the Bruins got another shot at the title and this time succeeded, defeating Duke 98–83.

During the next 11 years, UCLA knocked off nearly any potential challenger in its way. The Bruins went on to win 10 titles from 1964 to 1975. This included seven consecutive national championships between 1967 and 1973.

"Winning seven consecutive NCAA championships has set a gold standard in college sports that may never be equaled," said center Lew Alcindor, who was part of the winning 1967, 1968, and 1969 teams. "At the time it happened, I didn't think of it that much because I was still in my professional career, and frankly, was getting used to UCLA winning. But looking back, it's extraordinary for any sport to have one team consistently set the standard for excellence. I'm so happy I could be part of that extraordinary legacy."

> "Winning seven consecutive NCAA championships has set a gold standard in college sports that may never be equaled."
>
> —UCLA center Lew Alcindor

Only one team interrupted UCLA's dynasty. In 1966, Texas Western—which is now known as the University of Texas-El Paso (UTEP)—became a national story as the Miners made a run all the way to the national championship game. Going up against powerhouse Kentucky and its longtime coach Adolph Rupp, Texas Western became the first team to have an all-black starting lineup in the NCAA title game. In that game, the Miners pulled off the win to capture the championship.

Once the Bruins' run of titles ended in 1975, the door opened for others to step up. And in 1976, Indiana did just that. The Hoosiers knocked off four top-10 teams in the NCAA Tournament. That completed a perfect season as Indiana went 32–0 and became only the seventh men's team ever to go undefeated and win the national title. Through 2018, no team had accomplished this feat since the 1976 Hoosiers.

In 1982, the landscape of college basketball changed forever as the inaugural women's NCAA Tournament took place. The 32-team field came from across the country. Louisiana Tech took home the first NCAA women's title as part of a 54-game winning streak. In the process, the Lady Techsters set a new standard and helped pave the way for future generations.

"We were setting records and doing things way long before others were. We were visionaries," said Lady Techsters coach Sonja Hogg.

Whereas the women's game was blossoming in the 1980s and early 1990s, the men's game had seen different teams emerge through the years. But in the early 1990s, a new power began to take over. After winning its first national championship by defeating Kansas in 1991, Duke became the first team since UCLA to win back-to-back national championships. The Blue Devils defeated Michigan in the 1992 national championship game.

> "We were setting records and doing things way long before others were. We were visionaries."
> –Lady Techsters coach Sonja Hogg

Duke's titles came thanks to some of college basketball's greatest players in Christian Laettner, Bobby Hurley, and Grant Hill. This trio knocked off some of the nation's best teams, including the 1992 Wolverines, the Michigan team that had famously started five freshmen–Chris Webber, Jalen Rose, Juwan Howard, Ray Jackson, and Jimmy King, a.k.a. "the Fab Five." Starting a lineup with that much youth was a concept that was unheard of before 1992.

Tennessee's Chamique Holdsclaw (23) celebrates as the Lady Vols clinch the 1998 national title.

On the women's side, legendary programs were also starting to cement their legacies. Tennessee stepped into the spotlight in the late 1980s and stayed there for decades. The Lady Volunteers, led by Hall of

Fame coach Pat Summitt, won their first title in 1987 and continued to be a factor until she retired in 2012.

The most impressive Tennessee run came when the Lady Vols won three consecutive NCAA titles from 1996 to 1998. Behind All-American forward Chamique Holdsclaw and freshman standout Tamika Catchings, the Lady Vols capped off the run with a perfect 39–0 record during the 1997–98 season. The team became so popular that Tennessee had a higher average attendance than some NBA teams.

"The best team won the championship they deserve," Summitt said. "It has been such an incredible year, I cannot imagine them not getting what they deserved."

As the competition continues to grow, the Lady Vols' run at the top of the women's game has faded. Tennessee last won a national championship in 2008, but the Vols were the only team to appear in each NCAA Tournament from 1982 to 2018.

> "The best team won the championship they deserve. It has been such an incredible year, I cannot imagine them not getting what they deserved."
>
> –Tennessee coach Pat Summitt

(From left) UConn's Tina Charles, Maya Moore, and Renee Montgomery celebrate winning the 2009 national title.

As Tennessee slowed down, Connecticut took over as the team to beat. Under coach Geno Auriemma, the Huskies have gone on multiple winning streaks that have lasted more than 70 games. The longest streak came between 2014 and 2017. The Huskies won a college basketball-record 111 consecutive games.

One of the shorter winning streaks came between 2008 and 2010. Connecticut won 78 consecutive games and won NCAA championships in both 2009 and 2010. The Huskies featured one of their all-time great starting lineups during this period with future WNBA standouts and Olympic gold medalists Tina Charles, Tiffany Hayes, and Maya Moore leading the charge. Of the 78 consecutive wins, only just one was decided by single digits. That came in the 2010 national championship, as the Huskies knocked off Stanford by six points.

On the men's side, traditional powers such as Duke, Kentucky, and North Carolina continued to thrive, but new powers emerged as well. After a run to the NCAA title game in 2000, Florida went on to make the tournament for the next seven seasons. Then, in 2006, everything came together.

Behind talented sophomores Corey Brewer, Joakim Noah, and Al Horford, Florida came into the NCAA Tournament as a No. 3 seed. The Gators then made their way to the national championship game, where they dispatched UCLA to win the program's first national title. All three stars would go on to become first-round NBA draft picks, but first they decided to come back for another run at a college title in 2007.

The Gators stayed atop the polls all season. In the NCAA Tournament, Florida came in as the top overall seed and rolled to the championship game. This time, the Gators knocked off Ohio State to win back-to-back titles. Through 2018, they were the last men's team to do that.

Whereas Brewer, Horford, and Noah each stayed for multiple seasons with Florida, the one-and-done trend was quickly taking over, as many of the top players spent just one season in college before entering the NBA Draft. Relying on freshmen, even those with tons of talent, wasn't always easy. Coaches struggled to catch up. John Calipari raced to the head of the class. His Memphis team, led by freshman Derrick Rose, reached the 2008 national title game. Then Calipari took over the Kentucky Wildcats in 2009, establishing the school as the go-to place for one-and-done standouts.

The most memorable of Calipari's teams was in 2011–12. Behind standout freshmen Anthony Davis and Michael Kidd-Gilchrist, Kentucky went 38–2 and won the school's eighth national championship. Three years later, another young Kentucky team nearly became the first team since Indiana to complete a perfect

Nobody could stop Florida and its big three of Joakim Noah (13), Al Horford (42), and Corey Brewer in the 2006 and 2007 NCAA Tournaments.

season, but the Wildcats were upset by Wisconsin in the 2015 national semifinal.

While the one-and-done model has taken over much of the sport, other programs, such as Villanova in 2016 and 2018, have shown that you can still win a national championship using players who stay multiple years in college.

UCLA

CHAPTER 8

LEGENDARY COACHES

Although college players come and go in only a few years, coaches can last decades. The best ones not only recruit great talent and know their Xs and Os but also instill a culture and attitude in their program that help it reach new heights.

The sport's original coach was its inventor, James Naismith. After leaving Massachusetts, Naismith became a physical education professor at Kansas. He also became coach of the men's basketball team in 1898. Ironically, the "Father of Basketball" is the only Jayhawks coach in history to post a losing record.

UCLA's John Wooden wears a net for a necklace after the Bruins won the 1975 NCAA title.

Most discussions of great college basketball coaches start with John Wooden. Before he arrived at UCLA in 1948, the Bruins had never made an NCAA Tournament. Their record in nine seasons under their previous coach had been just 93–120. Yet Wooden led the Bruins to a conference title in his first season, and by 1950, they were in the NCAA Tournament.

That was only the beginning. Wooden coached the Bruins to 10 national titles, including seven in a row from 1967 to 1973. No other men's coach has won more than two in a row. Included in that stretch was an 88-game winning streak from 1971 to 1973.

But beyond the impressive wins, Wooden was a legendary leader. He developed principles such as the "Pyramid of Success." It outlined the journey to becoming a great player and a great person. These principles still influence head coaches today.

Unlike Wooden, Dean Smith did not inherit a struggling program. When Smith was promoted to North Carolina's head men's coach in 1961, the Tar Heels were coming off a conference championship. In Smith's first season, he went 8–9. But that was the last time he had a losing season. Smith's Tar Heels became a model of consistency. Starting in 1975, North

Carolina won at least 20 games in 27 consecutive seasons. It made the NCAA Tournament in 23 of them. Every year from 1981 to 1993, the Tar Heels advanced at least to the Sweet 16.

But Smith's greatest influence may have come off the court. When he took over the program, it had been placed under NCAA probation for rules violations. Smith also integrated the program in 1966, welcoming Charlie Scott as the team's first black player. And in 36 seasons, Smith graduated 96 percent of his letter winners. He retired with 879 career wins, the most all time at that point.

By sheer numbers, it's hard to top Mike Krzyzewski for coaching excellence. "Coach K" took over the Duke men's program in 1980, and by 2011 he had passed legendary Indiana coach Bobby Knight in all-time coaching wins. By the close of the 2017–18 season, Krzyzewski had 1,027 career victories. That was almost half of all wins in program history.

The Blue Devils won five national titles from 1981 to 2015 and made the tournament in 34 out of the first 38 seasons under Krzyzewski. Duke was especially dominant at home at Cameron Indoor Stadium. In 2000, the floor was named Coach K Court.

No Division I men's college basketball coach has won more than Duke's Mike Krzyzewski.

Krzyzewski and Knight shared connections beyond being successful coaches. Krzyzewski played under Knight at Army, and he eventually coached there himself before going to Duke. Knight, meanwhile, made his name at Indiana. The Hoosiers were a dynasty almost from the start of Knight's career there in 1971. They won 11 Big Ten Conference titles, and Knight became the winningest coach in Big Ten history in 1989. After a stint coaching Texas Tech, Knight retired in 2008 with 902 career wins.

But Knight was a polarizing figure. He was known for his temper, famously tossing a chair across the court during a 1985 game with Purdue. More seriously, allegations of player abuse followed Knight throughout his career. In 2000, a video surfaced of him choking a player in 1997, and Knight was fired soon after.

Few coaches are as connected to their schools as Jim Boeheim is to Syracuse. Boeheim was a walk-on player in 1962 who eventually became team captain. After a brief pro career, Boeheim returned to Syracuse as a graduate assistant to the men's team. He was promoted to head coach in 1976, two seasons after Roy Danforth had led the team to its first Final Four.

Boeheim managed to maintain a high level of success, missing the tournament only eight times from 1976 to 2018 (though some results were later vacated by the NCAA). Boeheim led the Orange to their first national title in 2003, with some help from forward Carmelo Anthony. Still coaching into his 70s, as of 2018 Boeheim sat third on the all-time wins list.

Although the women's game has a much shorter history than the men's, two coaches established themselves as the best of the best.

Pat Summitt was a physical education teacher at the University of Tennessee in 1974. She also happened to coach its women's basketball team. Her tenure actually preceded NCAA sanctioning of women's basketball. Before long, the Lady Volunteers were the NCAA's iconic women's basketball program.

Tennessee made the first NCAA women's Final Four and never looked back. Summitt won eight national titles and finished her 38-year career with a record of 1,098–208. Only once did one of her Tennessee teams fail to reach the NCAA Tournament Sweet 16. Plus, she graduated 100 percent of her players.

Summitt would stand alone at the top of the sport if not for Geno Auriemma. The UConn coach needed some time to establish himself. He took over the Huskies in 1985, and they won their first national title in 1995. After that, the sport's greatest rivalry took off.

Tennessee's Pat Summitt (left) and UConn's Geno Auriemma (right) built the two iconic teams in women's college basketball.

Auriemma eventually surpassed Summitt, leading UConn to 10 more national titles during the next 21 years. In 2017, he earned his 1,000th career win. That made him the fastest coach to do so, needing just 1,135 games. The Huskies also put together an absurd 111-game winning streak from November 2014 to March 2017, bookending a perfect 40–0 season. And like Summitt, Auriemma's players all graduated.

CHAPTER 9

GREAT UPSETS AND COMEBACKS

Each March, fans across the nation clamor for the magic of the NCAA men's and women's basketball tournaments. Between the upsets and wild comebacks that occur during these tournaments, there is enough drama to fill a soap opera. But when it comes to "The Tournament," upsets are what draw in even the most casual of basketball fans.

Before any 16 seed in the men's bracket pulled off an upset against a top-seeded team, it happened in the women's game in 1998. Behind strong offense and some untimely injuries for No. 1-seeded Stanford, Harvard knocked off the Cardinal 71–67.

Harvard players celebrate after the 16-seeded Crimson upset No. 1 seed Stanford in the 1998 NCAA Tournament.

Upsets on the men's and women's side happen every year. Even today, few compare with the 1983 North Carolina State men's team. Their run through the tournament helped establish the event as "March Madness."

After struggling in the regular season, NC State needed a strong showing in the ultra-competitive ACC tournament to make the NCAA Tournament. When the Wolfpack did just that by winning the ACC tournament, they earned an automatic berth into the "Big Dance." And then they kept winning. From there, NC State made a miraculous run to the NCAA championship game. Finally, with time running out, Wolfpack big man Lorenzo Charles dunked the ball to give his team a 54–52 win and a national championship over the heavily favored Houston Cougars.

Along with many upsets in the men's and women's tournaments, some of the top teams in the bracket have kept their seasons alive with amazing come-from-behind wins. Look no further than Illinois' 2005 Sweet Sixteen game against Arizona. Playing in front of a favorable crowd in Chicago, the Fighting Illini trailed by 14 points with approximately four minutes remaining. Illinois made an improbable comeback and won in overtime to advance to the Elite Eight.

Though there are plenty of memorable comebacks and upsets, here are a few that stand above the rest.

1968: UCLA vs. HOUSTON

Tagged as the "Game of the Century," this matchup was the first regular season men's college basketball game to be televised nationally. In front of a raucous crowd of more than 50,000 fans at the Astrodome in Houston, the No. 2 Cougars ended top-ranked UCLA's 47-game winning streak on January 20, 1968. The game went down to the wire, and Elvin Hayes sunk two free throws to put Houston ahead for good and knock off the Bruins 71–69. UCLA had won three of the past four national championships, including 1967, when it defeated the Cougars in the national semifinals. The Bruins would get revenge later that season, however. They knocked Houston out of the NCAA Tournament with a 101–69 win in the national semifinals.

1974: UCLA vs. NOTRE DAME

Six years later, UCLA found itself in the middle of another long winning streak. The Bruins entered this matchup after winning 88 consecutive games. But at No. 2 in the country, Notre Dame was no slouch. Led by 32-year-old coach Digger Phelps, the Fighting Irish

Chaminade's Tony Randolph (right) jostles for position with Virginia's Ralph Sampson in their 1982 game.

handed UCLA its first loss in 1,092 days as the Fighting Irish prevailed 71–70. Notre Dame celebrated as the crowd rushed the floor when the buzzer sounded. The Bruins' winning streak is still the longest in men's college basketball history.

1982: CHAMINADE VS. VIRGINIA

Division II Chaminade has made a tradition out of hosting Division I schools each year in the Maui Invitational. That's because the little school from Honolulu had so much fun hosting Virginia in 1982. At the time, Chaminade was not even an NCAA program. Virginia, meanwhile, was the nation's top-ranked team and featured star big man Ralph Sampson. So few had reason to notice when the two teams met for a series of exhibitions in 1982. Yet after losing to the Cavaliers by double digits in their first two meetings, the Silverswords pulled off a monumental upset and defeated Virginia 77–72 in front of a crowd of fewer than 4,000 people.

1985: VILLANOVA vs. GEORGETOWN

These two Big East Conference rivals faced off in the 1985 men's national title game. Georgetown was the No. 1 overall seed in the tournament and featured future NBA star Patrick Ewing. The Hoyas were heavy favorites to win it all. Villanova, meanwhile, was a No. 8 seed and came in with 10 losses. Despite the obstacles the Wildcats had in front of them, Villanova became the lowest-seeded team to ever win a national championship. The Wildcats made an amazing 22 of 28 shots from the field and stunned Georgetown with a 66–64 win.

1991: DUKE vs. UNLV

Before Duke became a men's powerhouse in the 1990s, the Blue Devils had to slay the dragon that was Nevada-Las Vegas (UNLV), which had beaten Duke 103–73 in the national final one year earlier. The Runnin' Rebels went into their national semifinal matchup against Duke on a 45-game winning streak and looked destined to repeat as national champions. The Blue Devils had other ideas. In a game that was tied 17 times and had 25 lead changes, Duke knocked off UNLV 79–77 and went on to win its first national championship and begin a run of back-to-back titles.

1994: NORTH CAROLINA vs. LOUISIANA TECH

Before Connecticut and Tennessee had their moments in the spotlight, Louisiana Tech was the class of women's college basketball. The Lady Techsters won the first NCAA women's title in 1982 and continued their run of excellence into the 1990s. Heading into the 1994 national championship game, Louisiana Tech was on a 25-game winning streak. But the Lady Techsters' thunder was stolen by upstart North Carolina, which was making its first Final Four appearance. The teams battled back and forth all game. With 0.7 seconds remaining in the game, Charlotte Smith drained a three-pointer to give the Tar Heels a 60–59 win and a national championship.

1997: CONNECTICUT vs. TENNESSEE

Up until 1995, the Tennessee Lady Vols had consistently gotten the best of the Connecticut Huskies. That all changed at the Final Four in 1995. Connecticut capped a perfect season with a win over Tennessee to give the Huskies their first national championship and helped kickstart this rivalry. In 1997, Connecticut was once again undefeated and at the top of the throne as the Huskies took on the Volunteers in the Elite Eight. Despite Tennessee coming in as a No. 3 seed—a low seed by its standards—the Volunteers extracted some revenge on Connecticut. Tennessee knocked off the Huskies and ended their season with a 91–81 overtime win.

2017: CONNECTICUT vs. MISSISSIPPI STATE

It's rare to call it an upset when a pair of No. 1 seeds meet in the Final Four, but in this case, it is more than applicable. The UConn women cruised into the national semifinals on a 111-game winning streak and did not look to be slowing down any time soon. Mississippi State, meanwhile, was playing in its first-ever Final Four and didn't appear to be a team capable of knocking off the big, bad Huskies. However, the Bulldogs took Connecticut to overtime. At the end of the five-minute overtime period, Mississippi State had the final possession. Morgan William dribbled, pulled up, and hit a jumper as time expired to give the Bulldogs a 66–64 win—and shock the basketball world.

2018: MARYLAND-BALTIMORE COUNTY vs. VIRGINIA

Thirty-six years after Virginia suffered a historic upset against Chaminade, the Cavaliers once again found themselves on the losing side of a historic matchup. Virginia entered the 2018 NCAA Tournament as the No. 1 overall seed. That earned them an "easy" first-round game against 16-seed Maryland-Baltimore County (UMBC). UMBC came from a small conference and had lost a game 83–39 earlier that season. There was little doubt the Cavaliers would cruise to victory, which would make No. 1 seeds 136–0 all-time in the first round of the men's tournament. But UMBC jumped out to a big lead, and the usually forgettable 1-vs.-16 matchup suddenly became must-see TV. The Retrievers continued to hold onto their lead and thwarted any Cavaliers comeback attempts as UMBC pulled off the historic upset and won 74–54. Though the Retrievers bowed out in the next round, they will always have the claim to fame of being the first men's 16-seed that knocked off a No. 1.

2018: NOTRE DAME vs. MISSISSIPPI STATE

In the national women's semifinals, Notre Dame slayed the dragon that was Connecticut thanks to a game-winning shot in the waning seconds from Arike

Notre Dame's Arike Ogunbowale celebrates her championship-winning shot against Mississippi State.

Ogunbowale. Two days later, the Fighting Irish were back at it against Mississippi State, who knocked out the vaunted Huskies in the 2017 national semifinal. Early on, it was all Bulldogs and they led by as many as 15 points in the third quarter. Notre Dame wasn't done yet, however. The Fighting Irish mounted the largest comeback in women's national championship history and put themselves in a position to pull out a win. In the final seconds, Ogunbowale added to her legacy with a dramatic buzzer-beating three-pointer to give Notre Dame its first national championship since 2001.

SYRACUSE
15

CHAPTER 10

TODAY'S GAME

For most of its history, college basketball has been a training ground for the pros. If you wanted to play in the NBA or WNBA, you played in college first. That started to change on the men's side in the late 1990s and early 2000s. Technically, there was no rule that said players had to go to college. And with stars such as Kevin Garnett, Kobe Bryant, and LeBron James skipping college altogether, that became a trend.

In 2005 that all changed. The NBA made a rule requiring players to be a year removed from high school before they can enter the draft. That effectively requires players to go to college for at least one year (though some players have instead gone to pro leagues in other countries). The rule has been coined by many as the "one-and-done" rule.

Freshman Carmelo Anthony led Syracuse to the 2003 national title and then entered the NBA Draft.

The regulation served its purpose for the NBA. Although players such as Garnett, Bryant, and James became stars, many other high school players did not. Teams were also drafting teenagers based on potential. But that left rosters filled with young players not yet ready for the NBA. For colleges, the rule also had some benefits. Namely, it ensured that the best players spent at least one season in the NCAA.

Some fans despised the rule, though. They yearned for the days when top players spent at least three years in college. That allowed fans to really get to know the players and watch them develop. Many argue the quality of play was higher back then, too.

Nonetheless, some schools adapted to the new reality better than others. At the top of the list is Kentucky. Some teams try to avoid one-and-done players, opting instead for players who can stay and grow with the program. Since John Calipari took over as Kentucky's coach in 2009, the Wildcats have done the opposite. He sells Kentucky as the best place to prepare for the pros. Then he specializes in molding those players into good teams, even if the roster has lots of turnover. The approach has been a success. Kentucky reached three Final Fours in Calipari's first six seasons. That included winning the 2012 national title. And with the Wildcats pumping out NBA stars such as Anthony Davis, Karl Anthony-Towns, and John Wall, top high school seniors continue to follow.

Since Calipari used this strategy, other top powers have followed suit. Duke and Kansas have brought in their own one-and-done players. The Blue Devils have found success with freshmen standouts such as Tyus Jones, Jalil Okafor, and Marvin Bagley III. Kansas, meanwhile, has brought in the likes of Andrew Wiggins. Other lesser programs have also had their share of one-and-done players. However, no one has been able to bring them in and build successful teams around them at the same rate as Kentucky.

Although the one-and-done strategy may be flashy, it's not the only way to be successful. Sometimes experienced upperclassmen trump talented freshmen. Look no further than the Villanova Wildcats. In 2016, junior Kris Jenkins hit a buzzer-beater to secure a dramatic win in the national championship game. Two years later, another veteran-heavy Villanova team won again. Though the Wildcats didn't have high-end one-and-done talent, the battle-tested squad thrived in the postseason.

Although the names on Villanova's roster might not have been as famous as those on other teams, the Wildcats found a strategy that made them as successful as any program during that period.

Much like Villanova, some of the smaller college basketball programs—called mid-majors—have found success by keeping together a core group of players for multiple seasons. Among those who have found success this way are Butler, Wichita State, Gonzaga, and San Diego State. Some schools, such as Butler and Creighton, have had enough success that they have been invited into higher-profile conferences such as the Big East.

Although the one-and-done rule results in some high-end talent leaving the NCAA early, another trend is helping replace them. More and more foreign players are playing college basketball in the United States. At the 2017 men's NCAA Tournament, more than half of the teams had at least one foreign player. Some had many more. Players come to the NCAA from as close as Canada and as far as Australia and Africa. One team at the forefront of this trend is Saint Mary's in California. The Gaels have become a home-away-from-home for Australian players. Their 2017 squad that made the NCAA Tournament had seven players from the land down under. In that same tournament, Baylor and New Mexico State faced off in a first-round game with a combined 10 players who were born outside the United States.

The foreign-born players trend follows a similar trend in the NBA. Men's college basketball is also following the NBA with its emphasis on three-pointers. The three-point line was first introduced in the college game in 1986–87. During that season, players made 21.5 percent of their three-pointers. In 2017–18, that number had jumped to 37.5 percent. Stephen Curry was on the forefront of this trend. He made a record 162 three-pointers for Davidson back in 2007–08. He's since gone on to set NBA records for three-pointers with the Golden State Warriors.

Another trend emerging in college basketball is games being held in unique venues. The men's Final Four made the full-time move to football stadiums back in 1997. Each year, upwards of 80,000 people pile into these domed facilities throughout the country to see college basketball's best and brightest on its biggest stage. These domed Final Fours have allowed for more fans to get into the stadium and watch their

North Carolina and Michigan State duke it out on the USS *Carl Vinson* as the sun sets in 2011.

favorite teams play in person. However, players have sometimes complained that the non-traditional sight lines make shooting difficult.

During the regular season, teams have also gotten more creative in their venue choices. Early-season tournaments take place all over world, including places such as Hawaii, the Bahamas, and Puerto Rico. Aside from far-away locations, other games have taken place in unconventional spaces. In 2011, North Carolina and Michigan State played each other on a massive US Navy aircraft carrier, the USS *Carl Vinson*. The game was held on the flight deck. Other similar games have been held to honor the US military.

While top men's basketball players began skipping college altogether, a new opportunity arose for the best women's players in the late 1990s. Although pro leagues had existed, none had lasted in the United States. The beginning of the WNBA in 1997 changed that. Now women, like men, can go on to long pro careers in the United States. Many women even play two pro seasons each year, one in the WNBA and one in Europe or Asia. However, this is in part because WNBA pay is much lower than that in the NBA.

Still, these opportunities have helped grow the overall talent pool in women's basketball. As that's happened, more programs around the country are able to compete. Gone are the days when Tennessee or Connecticut has a cakewalk to the national championship game. Baylor has won a pair of NCAA championships under coach Kim Mulkey. She was a guard on the Louisiana Tech team that won the first NCAA championship back in 1982. She was also the first woman to win a national title as a coach and player.

Other programs have emerged, too. South Carolina has become a perennial power under coach Dawn Staley. The three-time Olympic gold medalist led South Carolina to the 2017 national title. Fellow SEC member Mississippi State finished second in both 2017 and 2018. The Bulldogs also had the distinction of ending Connecticut's 111-game winning streak at the 2017 Final Four.

On both the men's and women's side, it's never been easier to keep up with the top games. Fans can now see nearly every game on some platform. The biggest games are broadcast on major television networks. Many more can now be seen on some cable channel or streaming service. Most of the big conferences have their own TV networks. If fans aren't able to watch a game live, highlights are readily available through websites such as YouTube and Twitter.

The way to watch college basketball is changing as quickly as the game itself. Rule changes have come almost annually and changed the way the game is played. The men's three-point line continues to be pushed back. The men's game also went from a

Fans line the street to celebrate South Carolina's 2017 women's national title.

35-second shot clock to a 30-second shot clock in 2015. Meanwhile, the women's game made a significant shift in going from two 20-minute halves to four 10-minute quarters in 2015.

Changes such as these have already had an effect, and there continues to be a regular discussion in the college basketball community about how the sport can be the best it can possibly be. With this dialogue in mind, it's safe to say college basketball will continue to evolve in the years to come.

STANFORD
CARDINAL
UCLA
BRUINS

COLLEGE BASKETBALL'S WINNINGEST TEAMS

Based on all-time wins through 2017–18.

TIMELINE

1891

Dr. James Naismith nails two peach baskets to the walls of the gymnasium at the International YMCA Training School (now known as Springfield College) to form the first basketball court. Naismith established the first rules of basketball in December.

1893

Senda Berenson adapts Naismith's rules for her women students and uses the game at Smith College.

1895

The first game between two colleges takes place in Minnesota between Hamline and the Minnesota State School of Agriculture (later incorporated into the University of Minnesota). Minnesota won 9–3.

1896

The first women's intercollegiate game takes place between Stanford and Cal in Berkeley.

1897

The Amateur Athletic Union holds the first national basketball tournament, in which some college teams take part.

1938

The NIT, the first postseason tournament specifically for college basketball, takes place in New York City. Temple beats Colorado to win the tournament.

1939

One year after the first NIT, the NCAA holds its first national tournament. Oregon wins the eight-team tournament with a 46–33 win over Ohio State.

1950

The CCNY Beavers become the only team to win both the NIT and NCAA tournament in the same season. But a subsequent point-shaving scandal overshadows their achievement and college basketball as a whole.

1966

Texas Western (now UTEP) becomes the first team to win the NCAA men's title with an all-black starting lineup, defeating the all-white lineup from Kentucky.

1972

The AIAW, having formed the previous year, holds its first women's national tournament. Immaculata College wins its first of three titles in a row.

1975

John Wooden wins his final men's national championship with UCLA and 10th in the previous 12 years. From 1966 to 1973, the team lost only five games, including three perfect seasons. The national tournament also expanded in 1973 from 25 teams to 32.

1982

Women's basketball becomes a sanctioned NCAA sport and holds its first national tournament. Louisiana Tech defeats Cheyney State in the final.

1985

The men's NCAA Tournament expands to its familiar 64-team field. Villanova wins the title as the No. 8 seed, the lowest-seeded national champion ever.

1986

A 45-second shot clock is introduced to the men's game.

1987

After various conferences experimented with it for several years, the three-point line becomes a rule for all schools.

1998

The Tennessee Lady Vols, under legendary coach Pat Summitt, become the second team—men or women—besides the UCLA men to win three national titles in a row. Tennessee caps off a perfect 39–0 season with a 93–75 win over Louisiana Tech.

2009

Summitt wins her 1,000th career game, the first coach in all of college basketball to do so.

2011

The men's tournament expands to 68 teams, now including a "First Four" round.

2017

The UConn women's team loses for the first time in 111 games, the longest winning streak in college basketball history.

2018

Duke coach Mike Krzyzewski wins his 1,099th career game, passing Summitt for most wins by any Division I coach.

THE WINNERS

MOST NCAA CHAMPIONSHIPS (MEN)

1. UCLA, 11

2. Kentucky, 8

3. North Carolina, 6

4T. Duke, 5

4T. Indiana, 5

6. Connecticut, 4

7T. Kansas, 3

7T. Villanova, 3

MOST NCAA CHAMPIONSHIPS (WOMEN)

1. UConn, 11

2. Tennessee, 8

3T. Baylor, 2

3T. Louisiana Tech, 2

3T. Notre Dame, 2

3T. Stanford, 2

3T. USC, 2

MEN'S HIGHEST ALL-TIME WINNING PERCENTAGE

1. Kentucky (2,237 wins, 688 losses, 1 tie), .765

2. North Carolina (2,206 wins, 781 losses), .739

3. Kansas (2,217 wins, 841 losses), .725

WOMEN'S HIGHEST ALL-TIME WINNING PERCENTAGE

1. Tennessee (1,344 wins, 320 losses, 2 ties), .808

2. UConn (1,118 wins, 298 losses), .790

3. Louisiana Tech (1,110 wins, 321 losses), .776

** Through 2017–18. Minimum 25 years in Division I.*

THE RECORDS

MEN

Through 2017–18

MOST POINTS IN A GAME

100, Frank Selvy, Furman (vs. Newberry), February 13, 1954

MOST POINTS PER GAME IN A SEASON

44.5, Pete Maravich, LSU, 1969–70

MOST THREE-POINT FIELD GOALS IN A SEASON

162, Stephen Curry, Davidson, 2007–08

MOST REBOUNDS IN A SEASON

734, Walt Dukes, Seton Hall, 1952–53

MOST BLOCKS PER GAME IN A SEASON

6.5, Shawn James, Northeastern, 2005–06

MOST POINTS SCORED BY A TEAM IN A GAME

186, Loyola Marymount vs. US International (140), January 5, 1991

WOMEN

Through 2017–18

MOST POINTS IN A GAME

60, Cindy Brown, Long Beach State (vs. San Jose State), February 16, 1987; Rachel Banham, Minnesota (vs. Northwestern), February 7, 2016

MOST POINTS PER GAME IN A SEASON

33.6, Patricia Hoskins, Mississippi Valley, 1988–89

MOST THREE-POINT FIELD GOALS IN A SEASON

141, Jessica Kovatch, Saint Francis, 2017–18

MOST REBOUNDS IN A SEASON

563, Natalie Butler, George Mason, 2017–18

MOST BLOCKS PER GAME IN A SEASON

6.4, Brittney Griner, Baylor, 2009–10

MOST POINTS SCORED BY A TEAM IN A GAME

149, Long Beach State vs. San Jose State (69), February 16, 1987

FOR MORE INFORMATION

BOOKS

Doeden, Matt. *The Final Four: The Pursuit of College Basketball Glory*. Minneapolis: Millbrook Press, 2016.

Kelly, Greg. *The College Basketball Book*. New York: Sports Illustrated, 2011.

Schaller, Bob. *The Everything Kids' Basketball Book: The All-Time Greats, Legendary Teams, Today's Superstars–and Tips on Playing Like a Pro*. New York: Adams Media, 2017.

ON THE WEB

College Basketball Experience
www.collegebasketballexperience.com

NCAA Men's Basketball
www.ncaa.com/sports/basketball-men/d1

NCAA Women's Basketball
www.ncaa.com/sports/basketball-women/d1

PLACES TO VISIT

COLLEGE BASKETBALL EXPERIENCE

1401 Grand Boulevard

Kansas City, MO 64106

816-949-7500

www.collegebasketballexperience.com

The College Basketball Experience hosts the National Collegiate Basketball Hall of Fame and is an interactive museum where visitors can learn as well as play.

NAISMITH MEMORIAL BASKETBALL HALL OF FAME

1000 Hall of Fame Avenue

Springfield, MA 01105

1-877-4HOOPLA

www.hoophall.com

The premier basketball hall of fame, the Naismith Hall of Fame honors all basketball influencers from history, including countless college players and coaches. Visitors can also view exhibits telling the history of the game of basketball.

SELECT BIBLIOGRAPHY

Branch, John. "A Little-Known University Stuns No. 1 Virginia? You Must Mean Chaminade." *New York Times*, 17 March 2018, https://nyti.ms/2DAJWg6.

The Editors of ESPN. *ESPN College Basketball Encyclopedia.* New York: Ballentine Books, 2009.

Fagan, Ryan. "Two Simple Rules: How the Shot Clock and the 3-Pointer Changed College Hoops." *Sporting News*, 15 April 2012, www.sportingnews.com/us/ncaa-basketball/news/2288263-two-simple-rules-how-the-shot-clock-and-the-3-pointer-changed-college-hoops.

Klosterman, Chuck. "The 50 Greatest College Basketball Players of All Time." *Grantland*, 2 Dec. 2011, www.grantland.com/features/the-50-greatest-college-basketball-players-all-time/.

Medcalf, Myron. "Roots of One-and-Done Rule Run Deep." ESPN, 26 June 2012, www.espn.com/mens-college-basketball/story/_/id/8097411.

Norlander, Matt. "From Kimble to Kemba: Ranking the 25 Best Individual NCAA Tournament Runs." CBS *Sports*, 8 March 2017, www.cbssports.com/college-basketball/news/from-kimble-to-kemba-ranking-the-25-best-individual-ncaa-tournament-runs/.

Powell, Camile. "U-Conn.'s Taurasi Is the Difference." *Washington Post*, 6 April 2004, Page D01.

Waxman, Olivia B. "The Surprisingly Poetic Origins of the Phrase 'March Madness.'" *Time*, 20 March 2018, www.time.com/5188345/march-madness-origins-word-phrase/.

"Where Basketball Was Invented: The History of Basketball." *Springfield College*, www.springfield.edu/where-basketball-was-invented-the-birthplace-of-basketball. Accessed 7 Sept. 2018.

Wilner, Jon, and Jeff Faraudo. "NCAA Basketball: How Cutting Down Nets Became a Championship Tradition." *The Mercury News*, 12 Aug. 2016, www.mercurynews.com/2013/04/04/ncaa-basketball-how-cutting-down-nets-became-a-championship-tradition/.

Wooden, John, and Jack Tobin. *They Call Me Coach: The Fascinating First-Person Story of a Legendary Basketball Coach*. Waco, TX: Word Books, 1985.

Woods, David. "Who Is the Greatest Women's Basketball Player Ever?" USA *Today Sports*, 16 July 2014, http://usat.ly/1miB6mP.

INDEX

ABOUT THE AUTHOR

Grant Mitchell is a former investigative reporter and lifelong college basketball fan. He studied journalism and played Ultimate Frisbee at the University of Minnesota before earning a master's degree at the University of Missouri. He now lives with his terriers, Todd and Ryan, in Eden Prairie, Minnesota.